SCHIRMER'S LIBRARY
OF MUSICAL CLASSICS

Anthology of Italian Song
Of the Seventeenth and Eighteenth Centuries

Selected and Edited with Biographical Notices by

ALESSANDRO PARISOTTI

English Translations by

DR. THEODORE BAKER

D1590554

BASSANI	GASPARINI
BONONCINI	GIORDANI
CACCINI	MARCELLO
CAVALLI	MONTEVERDE
CESTI	PARADIES
DEL LEUTO	PICCINNI
DE LUCA	RONTANI
DURANTE	SARRI
FALCONIERI	SCARLATTI
FASOLO	STRADELLA
TENAGLIA	

Book I . . . . . Library Vol. 290

Book II . . . . . Library Vol. 291

G. SCHIRMER, Inc., NEW YORK

BIOGRAPHIES OF AUTHORS REPRESENTED IN THIS VOLUME.

G. B. BASSANI.

1657–1716.

He was born at Padua in 1657; became *maestro di cappella* in the church of San Petronio in Bologna, and in 1685 accepted a similar position at Ferrara, where he died in 1716. He was entered as a member of the Philharmonic Academy of Bologna in 1677, becoming its president in 1682. He was also a member and the director of the celebrated *Accademia della Morte* at Ferrara. He was an eminent violinist, one of his pupils being Corelli; and likewise a very skilful organist and a distinguished and gifted composer, having written six theatrical works, besides thirty other vocal and instrumental compositions. His teacher in music was Father Daniele Castrovillari.—From an extremely rare work entitled *Languidezze amorose—cantate a voce sola*, etc., the songs "Dormi, bella" and "Posate, dormite" (fragments of the Cantata called *La Serenata*), and "Seguita a piangere, povero cor" (fragment of the Cantata *L'Amante placata*), were taken—three pieces in which natural grace and simplicity are united with deep emotion and exquisite artistic taste.

G. B. BONONCINI.

1672–1748.

A son of Giovanni Maria Bononcini (or Buononcini), the celebrated theoretician and composer already mentioned in Vol. I of our Collection, the date of his birth is in doubt, being given variously at 1672 and 1660. He attended the school founded in Bologna by Gian Paolo Colonna, and speedily gave evidence of his talent by publishing instrumental compositions, Masses in 8 parts, and other noteworthy compositions. Proceeding thence to Vienna, he was admitted to the court orchestra in the capacity of violoncellist. Here he wrote the opera *Camilla*, which had extraordinary success both in Vienna and at the Italian theatres, and later at the Haymarket in London. At Rome he composed, in 1694, the operas *Tullo Ostilio* and *Serse*. In 1600 he brought out at Vienna *La fede pubblica*, and in 1701, at Berlin, *Polifemo*. Being invited to London in 1716, Bononcini, under the protection of the Duke of Marlborough and others, and Handel, whose cause was espoused by the reigning family, became bitter rivals; their rivalry was the occasion of the proposition, that these two eminent composers, in conjunction with a third (Attilio Ariosto), should write an opera together, each composing one act. The libretto chosen was *Muzio Scevola;* Ariosto took the first act, Bononcini the second, and Handel the third. Handel's victory was decisive; but Bononcini's patron, far from being discouraged, heaped new favors on him, received him into his own house, gave him a pension of £500 and afforded him every opportunity for the prosecution of his musical work.—His downfall, however, was approaching, and was hastened by the story, which he was too proud to contradict, that he had appropriated a madrigal by Lotti and given it out as his own composition. The resulting loss of prestige was never made good. The date of his death is uncertain, but is assumed to be 1748.

The aria " Per la gloria d'adorarvi," which we print herewith, is from his opera *Griselda*, written in London in 1722; it has many fine effects and an agreeable and flowing melody.

GIULIO CACCINI.
1546–1614.

HE was born about 1546 in Rome, and was known under the name of *Giulio Romano*. From Scipione Della Palla he received instruction in singing and lute-playing, and had already distinguished himself in his art when he sang, in 1579, the part of *Night* at the celebration of the nuptials of Francesco De' Medici and Bianca Capello, in an intermezzo composed by Pietro Strozzi. The renown of this gifted Roman composer, who, in coöperation with Jacopo Peri, Monteverde, and Emilio del Cavaliere, had so large a share in the creation of the musical drama, renders it easy to dispense with a long biographical sketch. Only a few of his principal works will be mentioned : *Il Combattimento d'Apollïne,* on a poem by Bardi ; *La Dafne* and *L'Euridice,* on verses by Rinuccini ; *Il Rapimento di Cefalo,* on a poem by Chiabrera, written for the wedding of Maria de' Medici, the niece of Grand Duke Ferdinand, with Henry IV of France, which took place Nov. 9, 1600.—We may also add a collection of *Monodie, Canzoni e Madrigale* for solo voice, from among which latter the song "Amarilli" was selected by reason of the rare artistic treasures which it reveals. —The precise date of Caccini's death is unknown ; but one of his dedications establishes the fact that in 1614 he was still living in Florence, advanced in years. His daughter Francesca was a distinguished writer of music and the authoress of the celebrated ballet *La Liberazione di Ruggiero dall' Isola d'Alcina.* Francesca Caccini enjoys the honorable distinction of being the first lady who devoted herself, with brilliant results, to the study of musical composition.

FRANCESCO CAVALLI.
1599–1676.

PIER FRANCESCO, known under the family name of his protector Federico Cavalli, a Venetian nobleman, was born in 1599 (or, according to other authorities, in 1600), as the son of Giovanni Battista Caletti-Bruni, *maestro di cappella* at the church of Santa Maria in Crema. His patron, who was the sheriff of Crema, being transferred in 1616 to Venice, took the youthful Caletti with him, entertaining him with splendid hospitality at his own palace, and furnishing him with amplest means for the cultivation of his musical gifts. In 1617 he was received into the choir of San Marco, then conducted by Monteverde ; in 1640 he was appointed organist of the second organ of that cathedral, obtaining the post of first organist in 1665. In 1668 he became conductor of the ducal musical organization, holding this position until his death, which occurred on Jan. 14, 1676. He was an extremely fertile writer of opera, composing within the space of 32 years (1637–1669) thirty-nine dramas, all of which were successfully produced in the principal theatres. Cavalli continued Monteverde's reforms, imbuing his operatic works with greater breadth and power by means of increased variety of harmonization, the definitive establishment of the string-band, development of dramatic effect and rhythmic intensity. In 1660 he was summoned to France by Cardinal Mazarin, to assist at the nuptials of Louis XIV and Maria Theresa of Spain, on which occasion he brought out his "festival opera" *Serse* (Nov. 22), though with poor success, owing either to the then prevailing ignorance of the Italian language in France, or to a lack of musical culture at the French court. The introduction of the *Aria* into opera has been ascribed to Cavalli, but wrongly, for Monteverde has a prior claim to the merit of this innovation. Nevertheless, Cavalli gave the aria greater freedom and elegance of form, developing it artistically on the lines laid down by Monteverde. The arias in *Giasone* (Teatro San Cassiano, Venice, 1649), *Didone* (1641), *Serse* (1654), and *Romilda* (1651), are noteworthy examples of their class. *Giasone* (Jason), the most successful of his operas, from which the aria "Delizie contente" is taken, was produced with extraordinary applause first in Venice, then in Florence (1651), Bologna (1652), Naples (1653), Rome (1654), Vicenza (1658), Ferrara (1659), Genoa (1661), Milan (1662), and finally returned, with equal success, to Venice in 1666. At his death, Cavalli was the possessor of a considerable fortune, a portion of which he left to the descendants of his patron, and the remainder to certain religious foundations in Venice ; he had no direct heirs, his wife and his two sisters having died before him.

MARCO ANTONIO CESTI.
1620–1669.

THE aria "Tu mancavi a tormentarmi" is worthy of special notice, among Cesti's compositions, on account of the interesting variety which it exhibits. The author of *Orontèa*, of whom mention is made on p. VI of Vol. I of this series, was born at Arezzo (or Florence?) about 1620 ; he was a pupil of Carissimi and, in 1646, *maestro di cappella* at Florence ; in 1660 he was admitted to the papal choir. He subsequently became *maestro di cappella* at the court of Emperor Leopold I. He died at Venice in 1669.

ARCANGELO DEL LEUTO.
15——16—.

THE charmingly suave song "Dimmi, Amor," accompanying this sketch, is attributed to Arcangelo Del Leuto, concerning whom no positive facts could be found. The appended biographical notice consequently rests upon induction alone. Pietro Della Valle, the author of the poem *Carro di fedeltà d'amore*, which was set to music by Paolo Quagliati, inserted, in the *Trattato di Musica scenica* by G. B. Doni, a lecture of his own entitled *Della Musica dell' età nostra*. In this essay he mentions a certain Cavalier Del Leuto as an esteemed composer and player in Rome, together with Gio. Francesco Del Leuto, both highly skilled musicians ; these two names cannot have been used to designate one and the same person. He also speaks of G. F. Del Leuto as one of the interpreters of the *Carro*. Now, this *Carro di fedeltà* was printed at Rome by Robletti in 1611 ; consequently, it must have been given in some subsequent year—that is, early in the 17th century. In respect to both poetry and music, the style of our song would indicate that it belongs to precisely that period. It is therefore very probable that it was composed by Gio. Francesco Del Leuto, who, by reason of his virtuosity in playing the lute, first assumed the cognomen of Arcangelo, by which he may have been best known later on from its appropriateness in expressing his masterly command of the instrument. In the absence of any certain data, these more or less plausible conjectures are offered ; authoritative statements regarding this amiable lutenist would be gratefully received. In any event, "Dimmi, Amor" is unquestionably a piece of most delicate workmanship, wherein refinement of taste is wedded to moving effect.

S. DE LUCA.
15——16—.

THE arietta "Non posso disperar," which was discovered among old manuscripts of the 17th century, exhibits very noteworthy features in its leading and harmonization; its construction is remarkable for elegance, fluency, and pleasing effects. Despite most patient research, it was impossible to obtain data concerning this composer, who is ignored by the biographers of musicians. Probabilities, however, favor the assumption that he was a Neapolitan by birth, and lived in the first half of the 17th century.

FRANCESCO DURANTE.

1684–1755.

A PUPIL of Alessandro Scarlatti, he became one of the most eminent composers of the 18th century, and the head of the Neapolitan school of music. He was born at Frattamaggiore, a village not far from Naples, on March 15, 1684. He was admitted to the *Conservatorio dei Poveri di Gesù Cristo*, and in January, 1742, was appointed professor at the Conservatory at Loreto, at a monthly salary of ten ducats (equivalent to 42½ francs), to replace Porpora, who had departed to Germany. He succeeded Scarlatti as professor at the Conservatory of San Onofrio, and numbered among his pupils the finest musicians of the period, such as Fiorillo, Guglielmi, Speranza, Sacchini, and G. B. Pergolesi. Though endowed with a less powerful imagination than his master, he was nevertheless highly skilled in the development of themes and the art of harmonization. His compositions are models of scholarly construction in the above particulars, and for the smooth and *cantabile* leading of the vocal parts. His manners were rustic and awkward, his mind cool and reflective, his soul simple and ingenuous. Although his compositions never brought him in a large income, he practised such strict economy that he was enabled to erect a chapel at his own expense in the church of S. Antonio at Frattamaggiore, which he dedicated to St. Michael, and in which he was laid to rest after his death, which occurred at Naples on the 13th of August, 1755. The tomb bears the inscription *Franciscus Durante—Cappellæ-magister—Musicæ fecit.*—Plain to negligence in regard to his attire, he took particular pains with his curled and scented wig, to prevent deranging which he always wore his cocked hat. He was thrice married. With his first wife he lived in incessant warfare, as she spent his meagre earnings in the lottery. The second, whom he dearly loved, and who had been one of his servants, he himself laid in her coffin. A few months later he celebrated his third wedding, with another domestic.

The *Prayer* and secular *Aria* accompanying this sketch are pieces well calculated to show, in their different genres, the skill and taste of their author.

ANDREA FALCONIERI.

15——16—.

THE musical library of the Royal Academy of St. Cecilia at Rome possesses a valuable work entitled *Libro Primo—di Villa-nelle—a 1, 2 et 3 voci—con l'alfabeto—per la chitarra spagnuola—d'Andrea Falconieri—napolitano—dedicate—all'ill.mo et rever.mo sig.r Card. De' Medici — in Roma — Appresso Gio. Battista Robletti 1616—con licenza de' superiori.*—This volume, also valuable as a fine specimen of typographical art, contains 17 villanelles for one voice, 11 for two voices, and 4 for three voices; in all, 32 compositions remarkable for their simplicity and elegance. The second villanella was selected for publication because it appeared best calculated for effective interpretation, and the most graceful of all; a facsimile is annexed.

Andrea Falconieri receives no more than a scant mention in Fétis' Dictionary, which does not even give his proper name; the other biographers ignore him. It may be conjectured that he was born near the close of the 16th century; for the dedication of the book in question commences: " Hav-

2 Chi v'ha fatto oscure
Pupillette belle
Che serene, e pure
Rassembraui stelle
Chi m'ha tolto i dolci rai
Dillo Amor se tu lo sai
Dillo, e sia quel che si sia
O disprezzo, ò gelosia.
    Vezzolette ij.

3 Non più sdegnosete
Rimirar vi voglio,
Ne più superbete
Soffrir tanto orgoglio,
Che veder s'io non v'offesi
Vostri rai di sdegno accesi,
Pupillette, è in giusto duolo
O ridete, ò io prendo il volo.
    Vezzolette ij.

ing resolved to give to the press these, my Musical works, Part the First of my feeble conceptions. . . .", and bears the date of March 21, 1616. In the National Library at Florence may be found the *Quinto Libro delle Musiche di A. Falconieri,* published by Pignoni in 1619—a rare and interesting work.

G. B. FASOLO.
16— -16—.

A VERY rare book in the possession of Dr. Oscar Chilesotti bears the title: " *Mistican-za di Vigna alla Bergamasca; il Canto della Barchetta et altre cantate et ariette per Voce et Chitarra.* "—From this work is taken the aria " Cangia, cangia tue voglie," which appears peculiarly adapted for publication in this collection by reason of its charming naturalness and spontaneity.

In Vol. XLI, No. 48, of the *Gazzetta Musicale* of Milan, dated Nov. 28, 1886, Dr. Chilesotti gives a few vague notes concerning Fasolo, and remarks on the rarity of the above-mentioned work, of which even Vogel, in his researches in the Italian and German libraries, could discover no second exemplar. It was published in Rome by Robletti, in 1627. Biographers in general make no mention of Fasolo; but on p. 480 of A. W. Ambros' History of Music (Leipzig, Leuckart, 1881) he is noticed as "a Franciscan monk in a monastery at Padua, whose *Annuale Organistico* was published in 1645 at Venice," the excellence of whose musical workmanship shows him to have been closely related (intellectually) to Frescobaldi.

FRANCESCO GASPARINI.
1665–1737.

ACCORDING to Fétis, Grove, and Reiss-mann, he was born at Lucca in 1665; according to Florimo, at Camaiore near Lucca, in 1665; according to Riemann's Dictionary, and the *Annuario* of Paloschi, in the

latter place on March 5, 1668. He excelled as a writer of both sacred and secular music, and produced no less than 32 dramatic works, besides numerous cantatas, inter-mezzi, etc. The work upon which his fame chiefly rests is entitled "The Practical Harmonist at the Harpsichord" (*L'Armonico pratico al cembalo, ovvero regole, osserva-zione ed avertimenti* (sic) *per ben sonare il basso e accompagnare sopra il cembalo, spinetta ed organo*), Venice, 1683; an instruction-book in thorough-bass followed by Fenaroli in the compilation of his *Parti-menti.*

Gasparini's teachers were Corelli and Pasquini; among his pupils may be mentioned Benedetto Marcello, who dedicated some of his compositions to him, and wrote of him with the utmost veneration. He was a philharmonic academician, and professor in the *Conservatorio della Pietà* at Venice; later he was appointed *maestro di cappella* at the Lateran in Rome. The two arias here selected are fragments of his Second Cantata.

The weight of authority sets April, 1737, as the date of his death.

GIUSEPPE GIORDANI.
1743–1798.

THE family of Giordani, who was also known as Giordanello or Giordaniello, comprising his father, three sisters, and two brothers, formed a company which gave representations of comic opera in the smaller theatres of Naples. In 1762 this company traveled to London, and was received with great favor at the Haymarket Theatre. Giuseppe, however, returned to Naples for the purpose of prosecuting his studies at the *Conservatorio della Madonna di Loretto.* He afterwards rejoined his family in London, where he composed a *centone* entitled *Ar-taserse,* followed by a serious opera, *Anti-gono.* From 1744 to 1782, devoting him-self to teaching, he wrote only the *opera* buffa *Il Baccio* (by some erroneously attributed to his brother Tommaso), which was given in London with marked success from 1744 to 1749. Again returning to Italy in 1782, he composed a great number of operas for all the Italian theatres, as well as many pieces of chamber-music, among which latter was the aria here reprinted, wherein fine effects are happily wedded to flowing melody. In 1791 he was called to conduct the Metropolitan Orchestra of Fermo, and while there wrote a large number of sacred compositions. Fétis and the Marchese Di Villarosa make a sad mistake in confounding Giordanello with Carmine Giordano, who was born about 1690, and was likewise a master of the Neapolitan school. Other errors with regard to his birth and death have been masterfully confuted by Florimo, in his great work on the *Scuola musicale di Napoli.* There is an inscription in the Cathedral at Fermo, according to which *vixit annos LIV dies XXVI* and *decessit pientissimus—Pridie Nonas Januaris An. MDCCLXXXXVIII.* This inscription, worthy of credence from having been written for the solemn obsequies of Giordanello, celebrated in January, 1800, show with the most scrupulous exactitude that he was born on December the 9th, 1743.

BENEDETTO MARCELLO.

1686—1739.

THE autograph manuscript of Benedetto reproduced below in facsimile is dated Jan. 21st, 1713. The volume containing it, which is entitled *Cantate per camera—Poesia e Musica—di—Benedetto Marcello—composte per la Sig^ra Ricci dilett.*, is apparently the very exemplar intended for said *dilettante,* for whom both verses and music were written, it being elegantly illuminated in gold and colors. None of the biographical notices on Marcello mention, as far as I am aware, this work so valuable both from a musical and literary point of view. The fragment "Non m'è grave morir per amore" forms a part of the second cantata; it is replete with peculiar novelty and charm, and is noteworthy on account of the harmonic leading in the recitative.

Marcello was born at Venice on Aug. 1, 1686, and died July 24, 1739, at Brescia, where he held the position of *Camerlengo* (Chamberlain). Further notices concerning him may be found on p. IX of Vol. I of this Collection.

CLAUDIO MONTEVERDE.

1568–1643.

BORN of indigent parents at Cremona, in 1568, he early attained to musicianly renown, and was admitted while still very young to the court of the Duke of Mantua in the capacity of a viola-player. Here the *maestro di cappella*, Marco Antonio Ingegneri, gave him lessons in counterpoint, and when but sixteen years old he published a collection of *Canzoni* for three voices. In a brief time his mastery of his art became such that his fertile and daring genius inaugurated a series of the boldest innovations. He aided powerfully in bringing about the transformation of the medieval modes into the modern chromatic system, by adopting the dissonance of the dominant seventh in such wise as to exhibit the harmonic relation of the fourth degree to the seventh, and by endowing this latter with its true character as the leading-note, with a regular resolution to the tonic. This important fact—which his genius intuitively felt, perhaps all unconscious of the grand results which were to follow—finds gradual development in his books of madrigals; arriving at the fifth book, he no longer hesitates to take without preparation the *tritone,* the *chord of the fifth and sixth,* the *dominant seventh and ninth,* and the *diminished seventh.* Herewith the transformation of the tonal system was completed, and

Monteverde, profiting by his new system of harmony to continue his course as an innovator, created the forms of the *Aria* and *Duetto*, skilfully employing the resources of instrumentation according to the scenic situation, and developing the musical drama, properly so called, in an expressive and dramatic form. But the fame of this eminent musician is so great, that many words are unnecessary. We deemed it proper to emphasize one remarkable feature in the work of this great genius. The *Lamento di Arianna* which we print is a shining exemplar of his gifts as a composer; it is taken from the opera *Arianna*, brought out in 1608 at the court of Mantua, and in 1641 in Venice, it being the first melodrama produced at the Teatro San Moisè. The National Library at Florence possesses the manuscript of the entire *scena*, the principal part of which is given here; this manuscript appears to be the author's original.

Monteverde died at Venice in 1643; near the end of 1613 he was appointed *maestro di cappella* at St. Mark's; he was buried in the church *dei Frari*, in a chapel to the right of the choir.

PIER DOMENICO PARADIES.

1710–1792.

This distinguished composer and excellent player on the harpsichord was born at Naples, where he studied under Porpora. He wrote *Alessandro in Persia*, performed in Lucca in 1738; *Il Decreto del fato*, given at Venice in 1740; *La Muse in gara*, a cantata represented at the *Conservatorio de' Mendicanti* in Venice in the same year. In 1747, he took up his permanent residence in London, and on December 17 of that year he brought out the opera *Fetonte* at the King's Theatre, which was given nine times with indifferent success. After this he abandoned composition, devoting himself to teaching the harpsichord; in his ca-

pacity as a teacher he regained his laurels by publishing the *Studies and Sonatas*. Clementi and Cramer used his works with great benefit to themselves. Cassandra Frederick, his pupil, played at the age of five and a half years, in a concert given at the Haymarket, compositions by Scarlatti and Handel, being the same who performed in 1760, in the double capacity of an organist and singer, the celebrated oratorios of the Saxon master.

Paradies returned late in life to Italy, and settled in Venice, where he died in 1792.

NICCOLÒ PICCINNI.

1728–1800.

Alessandro nelle Indie, a melodrama in 3 acts, set to poetry from the pen of Pietro Metastasio, was represented for the first time at Rome in 1758, and thereafter at Naples in 1774 and 1792. In the archives of the Royal College of Music of Naples are to be found 2 copies of this opera. One was donated to the College by Maria Carolina, and is in 3 acts; the other was among the autographs collected and acquired by Florimo, and has but 2 acts. The former is the score executed in 1758 and 1774: the latter is the same, revised and corrected, which served for the representations of 1792. The aria of *Cleofide* which we print herewith is one of the most salient numbers of the opera. The verses of the recitative were substituted, by Piccinni himself, for those written by Metastasio, but the aria following is that which is found in Act II, Scene 13, of the drama of the imperial poet. The form of this recitative, rich in dramatic features, the admirable construction, and the effectiveness of the whole composition, render this aria a veritable artistic gem.

Piccinni, of whom a further account appears in the first volume of this Collection, was born at Bari, on Jan. 16, 1728, and died of bilious fever at Passy, near Paris, on March 7, 1800.

RAFFAELLO RONTANI.

15——16—.

Le varie—musiche—di—Raffaello Ron-tani—a una, due e tre voci—per cantare nel cimbalo o in—altri stromenti simili con L'Alfabeto per la Chitarra—spagnola in quelle più a proposito per—tale strumento—in Roma—Appresso Gio. Battista Robletti, 1623—Ad instantia di Antonio Poggioli. All'insegna del Martello in Parione—Con Licenza de' Superiori.—The work bearing this title belongs to the valuable collection of the well-known cultivator of ancient music, Dr. Oscar Chilesotti, whose courtesy permitted it to be copied. The song so transcribed and harmonized is charming in its graceful simplicity, and forms a most sweet and admirable setting to Chiabrera's celebrated verses. Its composer was born in Florence towards the end of the 16th century, and was in the service of the Marquis of Capistrano, Antonio De' Medici, a natural son of the Duke Francesco Maria and Bianca Capello. He is mentioned by Quirinus van Blankenborg in his *Elements of Music,* who notices a book of *canzoni* published in Rome in 1632. The work by Rontani cited by Fétis in his biographical dictionary, and published at Florence by Zanobi Pignoni in 1614, may be found in the National Library in that city. The title differs very little from that heading this sketch, but it contains wholly different compositions.

DOMENICO SARRI.

1678–174–?

DOMENICO SARRI (or Sarro), was born of indigent parents at Trani, in 1678; his musical studies at the *Conservatorio della Pietà* in Naples were finished in 1697. In 1712 he was appointed vice-conductor of the Royal musical organization, and wrote an oratorio for the festival of San Gaetano. As early as 1702 he had composed a sacred melodrama, *L'Opera d'Amore.* He subsequently wrote many serious operas, and numerous oratorios, serenatas, comic intermezzi, cantatas, concertos for various instruments, and church-music. His *Didone abbandonata* deserves special mention; the music was set to verses by Metastasio, then a young man hardly 26 years of age, for the theatre of San Bartolomeo in 1724. This opera, which was enthusiastically received, was sung by the poet's friend Marianna Benti-Bulgarelli and Niccola Grimaldi (called *Nicolino*).—In 1741 Sarri was still at his post as first conductor; the precise date of his death is unknown.

ALESSANDRO SCARLATTI.

1659–1725.

IN the first volume of this Collection we published a few arias, full of grace and expression, by this distinguished and fertile composer. For this present volume we have again had recourse to him, and print herewith four more pieces in different styles. "Sento nel core" is a tender and expressive melody, extremely effective and not difficult of execution. The aria of *Tigrane* in the opera of the same name is a marvelous exemplar of its class in the truthful expression of feeling. In *Tigrane* Scarlatti tried, for the first time, the blending of the wind-instruments with the strings; and the harmonies of the horn, in the aria given here, are a most original device of the great Trapanesian. The little dialogue "Su, venite a consiglio," wherein the author feigns to converse with his own fancies and to listen to their reply, is replete with novel features. The canzonetta "Già il sole dal Gange" is spontaneous and genial. The annexed fac-simile is taken from a small manuscript volume of the period, in which the above-mentioned dialogue is also found.

For further notes concerning Scarlatti, the reader is referred to Vol. I.

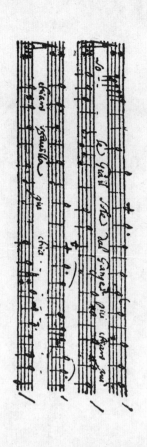
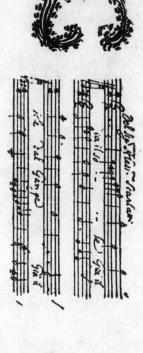
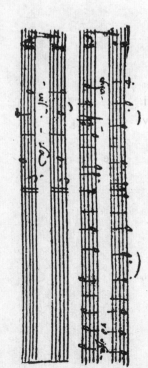
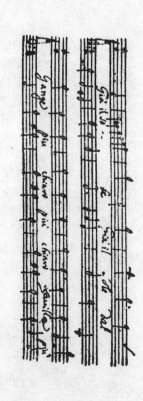

ALESSANDRO STRADELLA.
1645–1681.

"EVERYTHING IS obscure," writes Catelani, "in the life of Stradella." Although some give Venice as his birthplace, preponderant evidence shows that he was born in Naples about 1645. It is not known where and under whom he prosecuted his studies ; it is certain, that he speedily became a distinguished composer, and passed the greater part of his life as a musician at Venice. While there, he fell desperately in love with the flame of a Venetian noble, having been engaged by the latter to instruct the lady in his art ; in the course of this instruction he found time to lay siege to her heart, and this so successfully, that one night the pair fled together to Rome. The betrayed Venetian swore vengeance, and despatched two assassins to waylay Stradella ; but his purpose (so runs the legend) was this time frustrated in a most remarkable manner ; the assassins, going to church with the intention of murdering the musician after the performance of an oratorio composed by him, were so moved by the pathetic beauty of the music, that instead of carrying out their plan they disclosed it to their intended victim, who immediately repaired to Turin (1676), where he hoped to find efficient protection from further designs upon his life. But here, on a public promenade in full view of the populace, he was set upon by three hirelings of his implacable foe, and desperately wounded ; during his recovery he was wedded to the fair Ortensia, for love of whom he encountered such deadly peril. The wily Venetian, though twice foiled, persisted in his attempts, which were finally successful, Stradella being found murdered in his bed one morning in Genoa (1681?).

A fertile and distinguished composer, Stradella is also fabled to have been an eminent player on the harp, violin, and organ, and a facile writer of Italian and Latin poetry. At that period, but little music was printed in Italy, and besides, the unsettled life he led hardly permitted his attention to details of publication ; hence the major part of his works is still in manuscript. In Modena 148 of his compositions are preserved, among them being 6 oratorios and 11 dramas. In the library of San Marco in Venice there is a collection of 21 songs entitled *"Cante a voce sola dell' insigne A. Stradella legati alla biblioteca S. Marco di Venezia dalla nobile famiglia Contarini."* Of these, from which the song "Se Amor m'annoda il piede" is taken, a complete edition is in process of preparation. The aria "Ragion sempre addita" is from the *Serenata a tre voci;* this composition is noteworthy from the circumstance, that in it the orchestra is divided into two independent groups, called the *Concertino* and *Concerto grosso,* an arrangement also adopted in the oratorio reputed to have saved Stradella's life (*S. Giovanni Battista*). In this score a *contrabbasso* of small size appears for the first time.

ANTON FRANCESCO TENAGLIA.
16— –16—.

BUT few data are obtainable concerning this distinguished writer of music for church, theatre, and chamber, who was born in Florence early in the 17th century. He appears to have been the conductor of some choir in Rome, probably that at the Basilica of S. M. Maggiore. Certain it is, that he spent a large part of his artist-life in Rome, where, in 1661, he composed the opera *Cleano,* which was performed at the house of a personage whose name has not been preserved. In this opera is found indubitable proof that he was the inventor of the form termed the *aria with da capo ;* a form copied in 1686 by Carlo Pallavicini in his *Gerusalemme liberata*, and further developed by Alessandro Scarlatti, who has been erroneously credited with its invention down to this very day. It would seem that none of Tenaglia's compositions have been published, as in all my researches I have never met with a printed work by him, or discovered any notices of editions of his compositions at any time or place. Yet his music is extremely charming, picturesque, and effective, and is shown in the two arias given here, which are excellent specimens of chamber-style, and exhibit, considering the period at which they were penned, a notable advance as regards form. They were found in the Chigiana Library at Rome, which possesses not a few manuscripts of his in a crabbed and incorrect caligraphy. It is likely that others might be discovered in other Roman libraries, Rome having been, as observed above, the residence of this Florentine musician for many years; and it is hoped that these may also be published at some future time. —Under an old portrait of Tenaglia stands the legend : *Tenalia Florentinus musicus in rebus excellens.*

CONTENTS

Dimmi, Amor.
(Tell me, Love.)

English Version by
Dr. Th. Baker.

Cantata.

ARCANGELO DEL LEUTO.
(15.... 16...)

Dim-mi a - mor, dim-mi che fa La mia ca - ra li - ber - tà? Da che an - dò, co - me sai tu, A le - gar - si ad un bel cri - ne, Questo cor pien di ru - i - ne Non l'ha

Tell me, Love, tell me, I pray, Where my lov - er dear doth stray. Since he left me, as thou dost ken, By a stray fan - cy cap - tive tak - en, This poor heart so rude - ly for - sak - en Nev - er

4

11567

Non posso disperar.

(I do not dare despond.)

Arietta.

English Version by
D.r Th. Baker.

Andante grazioso. ($\bullet$ = 80.)

S. DE. LUCA.
(15... _ 16...)

Voice.

Non posso di - spe - rar,
I do not dare de - spond,

Piano.

non posso di - spe - rar, sei troppo, troppo
I do not dare de - spond, For thou art all too

ca - ra, trop - po, trop - po ca - ra, sei trop - po ca - ra al
dear,____ thou art all too dear,____ too dear un - to my

11568

8

11568

so - lo spe - ra - re d'a - ver - a gio - i - re, m'è un
on - ly hope so fond,__ The bliss - es of wait -ing, That

dol - ce lan - gui - re, m'è un ca - ro do - lor, ah,
soothe while cre - at - ing The pain they im -part, ah,

sì! m'è un dol - ce lan - gui - re, m'è un ca - ro do-
yes! That soothe while cre - at - ing The pain they im -

lor. Non pos-so di-spe - rar,
part. I do not dare de - spond,

cor; non pos - so di - spe - rar, sei trop - po ca -
heart; I do not dare de - spond, For thou art all too

ra,
dear,

sei trop-po, trop-po ca - ra, cara al
For thou art all too dear un-to my

cor,
heart;

Sei trop-po, trop-po ca - ra, ca-ra al
Thou art too dear, too dear un-to my

cor.
heart.

Vezzosette e care.

(Charming eyes so wary.)

Villanella.

English Version by
Dr Th. Baker.

ANDREA FALCONIERI.
(15.... - 16....)

Allegretto quasi Gavotta. (♩=104.)

Vez - zo - set - te e ca - re pu - pil - let - te ar - den - ti, chi v'ha fatto a -
Charming eyes so war - y, Eyes so bright and tender, Where-fore now so

va - re de' bei rai lu - cen - ti; chi v'ha fatto a - va - re de' bei rai lu -
char - y Of your ra-diant splen-dor? Where-fore now so char - y Of your ra - diant

cen - ti? Vez - zo - set - te e ca - re pu - pil - let - te ar -
splen - dor? Charming eyes so war - y, Eyes so bright and

den - ti, chi v'ha fat - to a - - va - re de' bei rai lu -
ten - der, Where-fore now so char - y Of your ra - diant

cen - ti; chi v'ha fatto a - va - re de' bei rai lu - cen - ti?
splendor? Where-fore now so char - y Of your ra - diant splen - dor?

S'io ri - mi - ro i vo - stri
When for kind - ly looks en -

Se bel rio.
(When the murm'ring.)
Canzonetta.

English Version by
Dr Th. Baker.

RAFFAELLO RONTANI.
(15... _16...)

1. Se bel rio, se bel l'au-
2. Se già mai tra fior ver-
1. When the mur-m'ring brook-let
2. When o'er crim-son flow-'ry

ret - ta fra l'er - bet - ta sul mat - tin mor - mo - ran
mi - gli, se tra gi - gli ves - te l'al - ba un au - reo
gush - es 'Neath the bush - es, And the morn - ing breeze be -
val - leys, Glist'ning lil - ies, Gold - en rays of dawn are

17

let - to___ bag-ni il   piè___ nell' on - de___ chiare,
mon-do,___ ri - de il   ciel___ quando è   gioi - o - so;
play-ing,___ Laves our   feet___ with gen - tle___ motion,
rene-ly,___ And the   laugh - ing skies   be - guile,

sì   che   l'ac - qua su___ l'a - - re - na scherzi a pe -
ben è   ver: ma non___ san   po - i,   co - me vo
When the   wave - let light - ly   dancing Sparkles glanc -
Tho' all   Na - ture may___ en - deav-or, She can nev -

na, noi di - ciam che   ri - de il ma - re.
i,   fa - re un ri - so   gra - zi - o - so.
ing, Then we say,___ how   smiles___ the o - cean.
er Match the sweet - ness   of___ thy smile.

Amarilli, mia bella.

(Amarilli, my fair one.)

Madrigal.

English Version by
D.ʳ Th. Baker.

GIULIO CACCINI.
(1546–1614)

Moderato affettuoso. (♩ = 66)

A - ma - ril - li, mia bel - la, non credi o del mio
A - ma - ril - li, my fair one, Canst thou thine heart to

cor dol - - ce de-si - o, d'es - - ser tu
doubt e'er sur - ren - der, Doubt of my love

l'a-mor mi - o? Cre - di-lo pur: e se ti -
true and ten - der? Do but be - lieve, for should e'er

mor t'as-sa - le, du - bi-tar non ti va - le.
fear as-sail thee It can nev-er a - vail thee.

Lasciatemi morire!
(No longer let me languish.)

English Version by
Dr Th. Baker.

Canto from the Opera
"Ariana."

CLAUDIO MONTEVERDE.
(1568–1643)

11572 r
Printed in the U. S. A

Delizie contente, che l'alma beate.

(Ye blisses, that ravish.)

Aria from the Opera
"Giasone."

English Version by
Dᵣ Th. Baker.

FRANCESCO CAVALLI.

(1599–1676)

De - li - zie con - ten - te, che l'al - ma be - a - te
Ye bliss - es, that rav - ish the soul of a lov - er,

fer - ma - te, fer - ma -
Give o - ver, give o -

- te.
- ver!

Su que - sto mio co - re deh più, deh
De - lights yet un - tast - ed Seek not, seek

più non stil - la - te le gio - ie d'a - mo - re, le gio - ie d'a - mo -
not to discov - er, Your trouble were wast - ed, your trouble were wast -

qui: non so più bra - ma - re, mi ba - sta co -
pire;   I long not for treasures, No more I de -

sì.
sire.

In
En -

grembo agli a - mo - ri fra dol - ci ca - te - ne
twin'd in Love's meshes, So soft beyond meas-ure,

mo-rir,_____ mo-rir mi con-
To die,_____ to die were a

vie - ne, dol-cezza o - mi - ci - da a mor-te,
pleas - ure; To mer-cies so ten-der, so ten - der

a morte mi gui-da, mi gui-da in brac-cio al mio be -
My life, my life to sur-ren-der, Em-brac-ing my heart's treas -

ne. Dolcez-ze mie ca-re, fer-ma-te-vi qui:
ure. Ye dearest of pleasures, Here let me ex-pire;

11573

E quando ve n'andate.

(O when will ye e'er leave me.)

Scherzo.

English Version by
Dr. Th. Baker.

ANTONIO FRANCESCO TENAGLIA.
(16...–16...)

Voice.

Quasi recitativo.

E quan-do ve n'an-da-te, spe-ran-ze a-du-la-
O when will ye e'er leave me? Ye shad'wy, de-lusive

Piano.

tri-ci al-la buon' o-ra? Non v'accor-ge-te an-co-ra
hopes, at last give o-ver! Why can ye not dis-cov-er,

oh-i-mè! che m'an-no-ia-te? e
well-a-day! How sore ye grieve me? O

quando,　e　quan-do ve n'anda - te?　quan-do, quan-do ve n'an-
when,　O　when will ye e'er leave me?　when,＿ when will ye e'er

da - te?
leave me?

Mosso. (♩ = 112)

Io più fia-to in
Not a　breath to

sen non ho da nu - drir＿ vo - stro de - si -
spare have I To in - spire your as - pi - ra -

re;　ri - sol - ve - te - vi, ri - sol - ve - tevi a par - ti - re, ch'io per
tions;　O de-part, de-part, and　end my trib - u - la - tions, For I

Risoluto. (♩ = 76)

voi mo-rir non vo', ch'io per voi mo-rir non vo'. Qual ca-
ne'er for you will die, for I ne'er for you will die. Where-fore

pric-cio vi man-dò a tur-bar la pa-ce mi-a?
hith-er must ye fly To dis-turb my peace of mind?

Voi siete Arghie pur la vi-a di partir non ri-tro-va-te. E
Ar-guses ye are, yet find No read-y way to un-de-ceive me. O

Recit. come prima.   cresc.   poco rit.

quan-do ve n'an-da-te? quando? quando? quando ve n'an-
when will ye e'er leave me? O when? O when? when will ye e'er

col canto

32

Quando sarà quel dì.

(When will the day e'er be.)

Strofette.

English Version by
Dᴿ Th. Baker.

ANTONIO FRANCESCO TENAGLIA.
(16... - 16...)

Con - to l'o - re ad u - na ad u - na co - me fos - ser
One by one, the hours I've count-ed As they pass'd like

an - ni in - te - ri: ma nel col - mo dei pen - sie - ri,
years de - spair - ing, But my fan - cy's flight most dar - ing,

ma nel col - mo dei pen - sie - ri tro - vo scar - sa
But my fan - cy's flight most dar - ing To the heights of

la for - tu - na. E se vi - ver si puo
hope scarce mount - ed. If for life one hope yet

rit. *p a tempo.*

più, ca - ra boc - ca, dil - lo tu; se a' ca - rat - te -
be, Mouth, be - lov - èd, tell it me: Shall the love - writ

ri di ro - se che sul lab - bro a - mor ti
signs so ten - der On thy ros - y lips e'er

11575

Tu mancavi a tormentarmi.

(Wilt no longer thou torment me.)

Aria.

English Version by
Dr. Th. Baker.

MARCO ANTONIO CESTI.
(1620-1669.)

42

Ragion sempre addita.

(How dearly are prized.)

Aria.

English Version by
Dr. Th. Baker.

ALESSANDRO STRADELLA.
(1645-1681.)

Ra-gion sempre ad-dita ad al-ma gen-ti-le che a-mata o scher-
How dear-ly are priz-ed True souls that per-sev-er, Or lov'd or de-

ni-ta lo sta-bil suo sti-le non can-gi, no, no. Io pur se-gui-
spis-ed, In faith-ful en-deav-or, Ne'er changing, no, no. It fol-lows, I

Se amor m'annoda il piède.
(If Love my feet enchaineth.)

English Version by
Dr. Th. Baker.

Cantata.

ALESSANDRO STRADELLA.
(1645 - 1681.)

11578

spe-ro, no, no, no, no, no, li-ber-tà non spe - ro, no.
free-dom,nay,nay, nay, nay,nay,There's no hope of free - dom, nay.

Un poco meno. (♩ = 84.)

Sian pur du - re le ca - te - ne, cre-scan sem - pre
Yet the fet - ters I — am wear-ing Still in-crease my

le mie pe - - - ne, cre scan sem - pre
woes de - spair - - - ing, Still in - crease my

le mie pe - - - ne, le mie pe - - - -
woes de - spair - - - ing,my woes — de - -spair -

ne: ch'in ser - vi - tù   co-stan-te, ch'in ser - vi - tù   co-
ing,   In slav-'ry e'er   con-fin-ing, In slav-'ry   e'er   con-

senza rallentare

stan-te   go-de o - gno-ra lan-guen - do un   co-re a - man -
fin - ing   And tor-ment-ing a heart,   love - lorn and   pin -

te,   go-de o - gno-ra lan-guen - do un   co-re, un   co-re a -
ing,   Tor - ment-ing a heart love - lorn, love - lorn and

man - te,   go-de o - gno-ra lan-guen - do un
pin - ing,   Tor - ment-ing a heart   love-

mf

11578

Cangia, cangia tue voglie.
(Change, O change thy fond wishes.)

English Version by
Dr. Th. Baker.

G. B. FASOLO.
(16... -16...)

11579

so.
ing.

Non t'ac - cor - gi, me - schin, che
Feel-est not, thou poor fool, she

sei fe - ri - to? La - scia, la - scia d'a - mar chi
will but pain thee? Quell, O quell love for her Who

t'ha tra - di - to; La - scia, la - scia d'a - mar chi
doth dis - dain thee, Quell, O quell love for one Who

t'ha tra - di - to.
doth dis - dain thee.

Sento nel core.

(My heart doth languish.)

Arietta.

English Version by
Dr. Th. Baker.

ALESSANDRO SCARLATTI.
(1649-1725.)

nel co - re, nel co - re, sen-to nel co - re
My heart___ my heart, doth languish,doth lan - guish

cer-to do - lo - re, cer-to_ do-lo - re, che la_ mia
Ev-er in an - guish, ev-er_ in an - guish, Hour by_ hour

pa - ce tur-ban-do va, ___ che la mia pa - ce
dwin - dles All peace for me, Hour by hour dwin-dles

tur - ban-do va.
All_ peace for me.

62

Splende u-na fa-ce che l'al-ma ac-cen-de, se non è a-mor-re,—— a-mor sa-ra, a-mor, a-mor sa-rà.

Hot flame and stead-y My soul en-kin-dles, 'Tis love al-read-y,—— Or love 'twill be, or love,— or love 'twill be.

Splen-de u-na_ fa-ce, che l'al-ma ac-cen-de, se non è a-mo-re,——
Hot flame and stead-y My soul_ en-kin-dles,'Tis love al-read-y,—

_ a-mor sa - rà, se non è a-mo-re,— a-mor sa-rà.
_ Or love'twill be, 'Tis love al-read-y,— Or_ love 'twill be.

Sen-to nel co-re
My heart doth lan-guish

11580

63

11580

Su, venite a consiglio.

(Hey! come hither, ye fancies.)

Dialogue between the Author and his Fancies.

English Version by
Dr. Th. Baker.

ALESSANDRO SCARLATTI.
(1649-1725.)

Su, su, su, ve-ni-te a con-si-glio, ve-ni-te a con-
Hey, hey, hey! Come hith-er, ye fancies, ye fan-cies, O

si-glio, o pen-sie—ri, ve-ni-te a con-si-glio, o pen-
come to be-guile me, Come hith-er, O come to be-

68

11581

Già il sole dal Gange.
(O'er Ganges now launches.)

Canzonetta.

English Version by
Dr. Th. Baker.

ALESSANDRO SCARLATTI.
(1649–1725.)

All'acquisto di gloria.
(To win glory.)

Aria from the Opera
"Tigrane."

English Version by
D.r Th. Baker.

ALESSANDRO SCARLATTI.
(1649-1725.)

11583

75

11583

ma, mi chiama, mi chiama il fragor, il fragor,
ing, are calling, are calling: "De-part, de - part!"

mi chia- ma il fragor.
Are call-ing, are call-ing: "De-part!"

Fine.

Dormi, bella, dormi tu?

(Art thou sleeping, fair one?)

Fragment from the Cantata

"La Serenata."

English Version by
D! Th. Baker.

GIO. BATTISTA BASSANI.
(1657-1716.)

Dormi, bel - la,
Art thou sleeping,

dor-mi, dor-mi tu? dor-mi tu? se
fair one, sleepest thou? sleepest thou? If

dor - mi so-gna-ti d'esser men cru - da, se
sleep-ing, be thy dream not all too cru - el; If

11584

Largo espressivo.

mor, e tu non fa - vel - li, ahi, bar - ba - ro a - mor, e tu non fa -
love, To mine ne'er re - pli - est, Ah, bar - ba - rous love, to mine ne'er re -

Tempo I.

vel - li ahi, bar - ba - ro a - mor.
pli - est: ah, bar - ba - rous love.

Dor - mi, bel - la, dor - mi, dor - mi
Art thou sleep - ing, fair_ one, sleepest

tu? dor - mi tu? se dor - mi so - gna - ti d'esser men
thou? sleepest thou? If sleeping, be thy dream not all too

84

11584

Posate, dormite.

(Sleep on, then.)

Fragment from the Cantata
"La Serenata."

English Version by
Dr. Th. Baker.

GIO. BATTISTA BASSANI.
(1657 - 1716.)

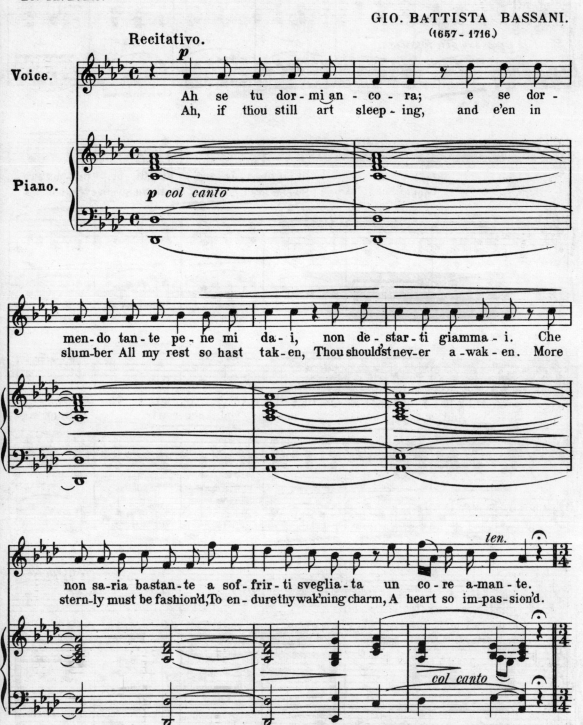

Ah se tu dor - mi an - co - ra; e se dor -
Ah, if thou still art sleep - ing, and e'en in

men - do tan - te pe - ne mi da - i, non de - star - ti giamma - i. Che
slum - ber All my rest so hast tak - en, Thou should'st nev - er a - wak - en. More

non sa - ria bastan - te a sof - frir - ti sveglia - ta un co - re a - man - te.
stern - ly must be fashion'd, To en - dure thy wak'ning charm, A heart so im - pas - sion'd.

87

11585

ra - te, e in pla - ci-do o - bli - o e in pla - ci-do o-bli - o dor-ma il
lov - ed; May kind - ly sleep ban-ish, may kind - ly sleep ban - ish All of

vo-stro fu - ror, ch'io par - - - to, ch'io par -
wrath thou might'st feel That I van - - - ish, I van -

- to, ch'io par - to, ch'io par - to, ch'io par - to, ch'io
- ish, I van - ish, I van - ish, I van - ish, I

par - to. Ad - di - o, ad - di - o.
van - ish! Fare - well, then, fare - well.

Seguita a piangere.
(Mourn with temerity.)

Fragment from the Cantata
"L'Amante placata."

English Version by
Dr Th. Baker.

GIO. BATTISTA BASSANI.
(1657 - 1716.)

No, non te-me-te, o pian-ti; ah non ve-
Nay, have no fear, my griev-ings, ah, mark ye

de-te che ri-de la pie-tà so-pra'l suo vi-so?
not how kind com-pas-sion smil-eth from her vis-age?

stan a for-za in bell' oc-chi or-go-glio ed i-ra,
Tho' her eye yet out-flash-es in an-ger and scorn,

sem-pre dal-la pie-tà cle-men-za spi-ra.
E'er of pit-y sweet clem-en-cy is born.

se-gui-ta a pian-ge-re, po-ve-ro cor, se-gui-ta a pian-ge-re,
mourn with te-mer-i-ty, pen-i-tent heart, mourn with te-mer-i-ty,

po-ve-ro cor.
pen-i-tent heart.

rit.

Recitativo.

Un ve-ro duol l'in-te-ne-ri-sce e mol-ce: io
To true re-morse her heart will sure-ly sur-ren-der, I

col canto

Andante. ($\quad = 60.$)

so di Fil-li il cor quanto sia dol-ce.
know that Phyllis' heart is warm and tender.

Se in-fe-de-le mi ha sof-
All the wrongs I've done, her

94

11586

Caro laccio, dolce nodo.

(Dainty meshes, net enticeful.)

Fragment from the
Second Cantata.

English Version by
Dr. Th. Baker.

FRANCESCO GASPARINI.
(1665 - 1737)

Lasciar d'amarti.
(Love's bond to sever.)

Fragment from the
Second Cantata.

English Version by
D.[r] Th. Baker.

FRANCESCO GASPARINI.
(1665 – 1737.)

Allegro moderato. (♩ = 84.)

Piano.

il basso legato e cantando — *f* *mp*

Las-ciar d'a- mar-ti per non pe-
Love's bond to sev- er, my heart to

assai rit.
a tempo

rit. con grazia *mf*

nar, ca- ro mio be- ne, non si può far, no,
free, Mine own be- lov- ed, it— can not be, no,

rit. con grazia.

ca- ro, non si può far; la- sciar d'a- mar- ti per non pe- nar, ca- ro mio
it can not, can not be, Love's bond to sev- er, my heart to free, Mine own be-

11588

Printed in the U. S. A.

Tempo I.

rar.
thee.

il basso legato e cantando

assai rit.

mf dol. e legato

Lasciar d'a - mar - ti per non pe - nar, ca - ro mio
Love's bond to sev - er, my heart to free, Mine own be -

a tempo

rit. con grazia

be - ne, non si può far, no, ca - ro, non si può
lov - ed, it_ can not be, no, if can not, can not

rit.

Per la gloria d'adorarvi.

(For the love my heart doth prize.)

from the Opera
"Griselda."

English Version by
Dr. Th. Baker.

G. B. BONONCINI.
(1672–1748.)

Per_ la glo - ria d'a_ - do -
For_ the love_ my heart_ doth

rar - vi vo-glio a - mar - vi, o lu - ci ca - re; per_ la
prize, O charmful eyes, I_ would a - dore ye; For_ the

104

11589

sì, nel mio___ pe - na - re, pe - ne - rò, v'a - me - rò,
vain, yet kneel___ be - fore ye. Love is_ pain, all in_ vain

lu - ci ca - re, pe - ne - rò, v'a - me - rò, lu - ci ca -
I im - plore ye, love is_ pain, all in_ vain I im - plore

re.
ye.

ff deciso.

Sen - za spe - me di___ di -
Hope - less 'tis___ to look___ for

letto vano affetto è sospirare, senza
kindness, Foolish fondness with sighs t'implore ye, Hopeless

speme di diletto vano affetto è so-
'tis to look for kindness, Foolish fondness with sighs

spirare, mai vostri dolci rai chi vagheggiar può
t'implore ye; But who-e'er might woo your gaze, Bask in your sunny

mai e non, e non vamare?
rays, and not, and not adore ye?

Sen corre l'agnelletta.

(As when a lamb confiding.)

Canzonetta.

English Version by
Dr. Th. Baker.

DOMENICO SARRI.
(1678-1740.)

del__ pa - sto - re, nè__ sa da__ lui__ par - tir:
shep - herd's call,__ Nor__ e'er from him will__ part:

Quel
Thy

lab-bro che m'al - let - ta di - spor può del mio co - re, di-
lips so sweet-ly guid-ing Con - trol my will-ing heart,__ con-

spor può del mio co - re a vi - ve - re, a mo - rir, quel
trol my will-ing heart, May life or__ death__ be - fall! Thy

labbro che m'al - let - -ta di - spor può del mio co- -re a

lips so sweet-ly guid- -ing, Con -trol my will-ing heart,___ May

vi - ve - re, a mo - rir,___ a vi - ve - re, a mo - rir, a

life or death be - fall,___ may life or death be - fall, may

vi - ve - re, a mo - rir.

life___ or death___ be - fall!

Sen

As

Sen cor - re l'a - gnel - let - ta al cen - no del pa - sto - re, nè
As when a lamb con - fid - ing O - beys the shep - herd's call,__ Nor

sa,__ nè sa,__ nè sa da lui par - ti - re, nè__ sa da_lui par -
e'er,__ nor e'er,__ nor e'er from him will part, nor e'er from him will

rit. *a tempo.*

l.h.

rit. *a tempo.*

tir; al cen - no del_ pa - sto - re, nè_ sa da_lui_ par - tir.
part; o - beys the shep - herd's call,__ nor e'er from him will part.

ten. *f* *rall. molto.* *a tempo.*

ten. *f rall.* *a tempo.*

f

dim. *rall.*

Vergin, tutto amor.

(Virgin, fount of love.)

Preghiera.

English Version by
Dr. Th. Baker.

FRANCESCO DURANTE.
(1684–1755.)

Ver - gin, tut - to a - mor, o ma - dre di bon - ta - de, o ma - dre pi - a, ma - dre
Vir - gin, fount of love, Dear Moth - er, thou of mer - cy, whose heart was riv - en, whose heart was

_so, pie-to- _so quel tuo cor, quel   tuo   cor.   O ma-dre di_bon-
_on high,_un-to_ thy throne_   on high.   O mother thou of

ta - de, Ver - gin, tut - to a_   _mor,   o ma-dre di_bon-
mer-cy, Vir - gin, fount of   love,   O moth-er thou of

ta - de,   o Ver - gin, tut - to a - mo - re, Ver-gin, tut-to a-mor,_
mer - cy,   O Vir - gin, fount of   love, O Vir - gin, fount of love,_

_ a - mor.
_ of love.

Danza, danza, fanciulla gentile.

(Dance, O dance, maiden gay.)

Arietta.

English Version by
Dr Th. Baker.

FRANCESCO DURANTE.
(1684–1755.)

11592 r

Gi - ra leg - ge - ra, sot - ti -
Light-ly and air - i - ly fly___

le al suo - - no, al
While bound - - ing, re - - sound - -

suo - no del - l'on - de_ del_ mar.
ing the bil - lows out - ring!

Sen - ti il
Dost thou

va - go ru - mo - re del - l'au - ra scher - zo - sa che par - la al_
hear the low voic - es of breez_ es soft blending Ap - peal to_ thy_

119

11592

Non m'è grave morir per amore.

(For my love thus to die.)

Fragment from a Cantata.

English Version by
Dr. Th. Baker.

BENEDETTO MARCELLO.
(1686 - 1739.)

11593

123

11593

de, che sa - reb - be mia pro - spe - ra sor - te soffri - re la
ish; O how welcome were death, if in dy - ing, To my gaze re-

mor - te, s'u - no sguar - do mi das - se in mer - ce - - de, mi
ply - ing, Came one glance from the eyes that I cher - - - ish, the

das - se in merce - - de.
eyes that I cher - ish.

Non m'è gra - ve morir per a - mo - re: sol
For my love thus to die noth - ing daunts me, Yet

M'ha preso alla sua ragna.

('Tis Love, that rogue so wily.)

Arietta.

English Version by
D.ʳ Th. Baker.

PIER DOMENICO PARADIES.
(1710 - 1792.)

Allegretto mosso. (♩ = 76.)

1. M'ha preso al-la sua ra-gna, m'ha preso al-la sua
dormo a-mor mi de-sta, s'io dormo a-mor mi
guido il gregge al mon-te, se guido il gregge al
mor tra mil-le pe-ne, a-mor tra mil-le

1. 'Tis Love, that rogue so wil-y, 'Tis Love, that rogue so
sleep doth Love me wak-en, From sleep doth Love me
fol-lows on the moun-tain, Love fol-lows on the
cru-el ar-rows hurl-ing, His cru-el ar-rows

Caro mio ben.

(Thou, all my bliss.)

Arietta.

English Version by
Dr. Th. Baker.

GIUSEPPE GIORDANI. (GIORDANELLO.)
(1743 - 1798.)

Ca - ro mio ben, cre - di - mi al - men, sen - za di te lan-guisce il
Thou, all my bliss, Be - lieve but this: When thou art far My heart is

cor___
lorn.___ ca - ro mio ben, sen - za di te lan - gui - sce il
Thou, all my bliss, When thou art far_ My_ heart_ is

Se il ciel mi divide.
(Since Heaven has torn me.)

Scena and Aria from the Opera
"Alessandro nelle Indie."

English Version by
Dr. Th. Baker.

NICCOLÒ PICCINNI.
(1728-1800.)

Por - ro dun - que mo - rì. Dun - que per - du - to tut - to è per
Then 'tis true, he is dead. With him then all is lost, too, for

me! Do - ve tro - var ri - po - so sen - za l'a - ma - to
me! Where shall I find re - pose when he, my be - lov'd, is

be - ne?
ab - sent?

Recit.

E questo il no-do so-spi-ra - to da
Is this the union that so long we have

no - i? Que-sta è la pa - ce? Que-sto il re-gno fe -
sigh'd for? This our con-tent-ment, and this our hap-py

Allegro vivace. (= 138.)

li - ce?
em - pire?

136

11596

Andante. (♩ = 63.)

sen - te il mio bel Nu-me? | Ah ch'io più nol ve -
dear all my soul pos - sess-es? | I shall see him no

Recit.

drò! | Bar - ba - re stel-le! Cle-o-fi-de in-fe -
more! | Des-ti - ny cru-el! Cle-o-fi-de un-

li - ce! Al - me-no ac - can - to del ca - ro be - ne;
hap - py! Were he but near me, Mine own be - lov - ed;

Ah! | ah! m'in-ter - rom - pe il pian - to.
Ah! Andante. | He nev - er - more can hear me!

138

11596

tir,   per - chè non m'uc - ci - de pie - to - - - -
neath,   why do not I per - ish my sor - - - -

- - so il mar - tir?   Di - vi - sa un mo -
- - rows be - neath?   Di - vid - ed one

men - to   dal dol - ce - te - so - ro,   non vi - vo,   non
mo - ment   From him,   my heart's treasure,   I live not,   I

mo - ro,   non vi - vo,   non vi - vo,   non mo - ro,
die not,   I live not,   I die not,   I die not,

145

11596

SCHIRMER'S LIBRARY
of Musical Classics

VOCAL STUDIES AND EXERCISES
SERIES ONE

The Library Volume Number is given in brackets: [453]

ABT, F.

Op. 474. **Practical Singing Tutor.** For all Voices (Spicker).

For Soprano or Tenor. Complete [453] ... 2.00
  Part I: Production of Tone. Intervals [454] .75
  Part II: Exercises for the Cultivation of Fluency [455] .75
  Part III: 20 Solfeggi [456] .75
  Part IV: 12 Exercises on Vocalization [457] .75

For Mezzo-Soprano or Alto. Complete [458] 2.00
  Part I: Production of Tone. Intervals [459] .75
  Part II: Exercises for the Cultivation of Fluency [460] .75
  Part III: 20 Solfeggi [461] .75
  Part IV: 12 Exercises on Vocalization [462] .75

For Baritone or Bass. Complete [463] 2.00
  Part I: Production of Tone. Intervals [464] .75
  Part II: Exercises for the Cultivation of Fluency [465] .75
  Part III: Solfeggi and Exercises on Vocalization [466] .75

BEHNKE, E., & PEARCE, C. W.

30 Voice-Training Exercises.
For Soprano [1090] 1.25
For Mezzo-Soprano [1091] 1.25
For Alto [1092] 1.25
For Tenor [1093] 1.25
For Baritone [1094] 1.25
For Bass [1095] 1.25

BONA, P.

Rhythmical Articulation. A Complete Method [1170] 1.00

BONOLDI, F.

Exercises in Vocalization.
Sop. [117]; M.-Sop. [118]; Alto [119] .75

BORDOGNI, M.

25 Easy Vocalises in Progressive Order [82] 1.00
36 Vocalises in Modern Style (Spicker)
For Soprano [432] 2.50
For Mezzo-Soprano or Baritone [433] 2.50

CONCONE, J.

Op. 9. **50 Lessons.** H [1468]; M [242]; L [243] 1.25
Op. 10. **25 Lessons.** M [244]; L [246] 1.00

CONCONE, J.—*Continued*

Op. 11. **30 Daily Exercises.** H [294]; L [555] . 1.00
Op. 12. **15 Vocalises.** Finishing Studies. H [275]; M or L [276] 1.00
Op. 17. **40 Lessons.** Alto [247]; Bass or Bar. [248] 1.50
The School of Sight-Singing. Practical Method for Young Beginners (Lütgen) [245] . 1.25

DANNHÄUSER, A. L.

Solfège des Solfèges.
Bk. I [1289]; Bk. II [1290]; Bk. III [1291].ea. 1.00
The same. sp. Bk. I [1085] 1.00

ESLAVA, D. H.

Método de Solféo (Carrillo). sp. Complete [1366] 1.50
The same. Bk. I [1376]; Bk. II [1377]; Bk. III [1378]; Bk. IV [1379] ea. .60

LAMPERTI, F.

The Art of Singing [1587] 1.00
Daily Exercises in Singing [570] .75
Vocal Studies in Bravura (Liebling) [1633] 1.00

LAMPERTI, G. B.

30 Preparatory Vocalises. Sop. [568] 1.25
29 Preparatory Vocalises. Alto [569] 1.25

LÜTGEN, B.

Vocalises (Spicker).
Bk. I: 20 Daily Exercises. H [654]; M [655]; L [656] .75
Bk. II: 20 Operatic Vocalises. M [930]; .75

MARCHESI, M. C.

Op. 1. **Elementary Progressive Exercises** [384] 1.00
Op. 2. **24 Vocalises for Soprano or Mezzo-Soprano** [391] 1.00
Op. 3. **24 Vocalises for Soprano** [597] 1.50
Op. 21. **The Art of Singing.** Bk. I: Elementary and Graduated Exercises [793]; Bk. II: 30 Vocalises for Mezzo-Soprano [794] ea. 1.00
Op. 32. **30 Vocalises** (Liebling) H or M [126]. 1.25

(Languages of texts are shown in small letters: e.= English; i.= Italian; sp.= Spanish. Where there is no other indication, texts are in English only. Other abbreviations used: H= High; M= Medium; L= Low; Bar.= Baritone; M.-Sop.= Mezzo-Soprano; Sop.= Soprano; Ten.= Tenor.)

Any Schirmer Library volume may be obtained in cloth binding. Prices will be quoted on request.
Prices Subject to Change Without Notice.

G. SCHIRMER, INC.   NEW YORK

A-1026